Ruminations of a Daydreamer.

Mitali Syamal

BookLeaf Publishing

Presentation by *BookLeaf Publishing*

Web: www.bookleafpub.com

E-mail: info@bookleafpub.com

ISBN: 9789357616577

First edition 2022

ACKNOWLEDGEMENT

I would like to acknowledge my family, close friends, well-wishers and work colleagues, with whom my frequent and daily interactions served as resourceful intimations for this book.

PREFACE

Short, curious, rhythmic insights into my world, what intrigues me, what fascinates and captivates me, even haunts me on a daily basis at this quarter of my life. A collection of short excerpts for me to look back on and wonder why it mattered at the time, and how things important to us change as we age: perspectives change, what captures our interests also change. We as humans are not stagnant in our thoughts and desires, similarly, this book captures the fleeting moments of introspection fed into bursts of spontaneous creativity expressed poetically for the enjoyment of others who might find they are not alone in their thoughts.

I am my own Prison.

Looking for someone,
Or something,
To save me from this
Abyss of despair.

On the surface
Appear I
Sound, and clean
Unbeknownst to others.

A bystander to
All, and sundry,
Inner demons
Chaining, and caging me.

Surrender I
To oppressive thoughts.
Never meeting all
Expectations.

The biggest enemy --
My mind -- to be
Conquered so perception
Is not distortion.

Tomorrow will I
Resume the good,
Away with the bad,
A false promise.

Waiting for a
Reason to instil
Self care and
Preservation again.

None to impress, the
Joy of life fleeting
If sought in
Materialism.

Sinning away from
Aristotelian
Virtues, crying for order
For purity.

The Advent of Spring.

The sea of light
A cacophony of rays,
Shooting through
My bedroom window.

Light refracting,
Catching the condensation
Off the glistening
Framed windows.

Spring enters
With birds, flies, bees.
Dewy humid rains
Trickling on skins.

All crawling out
From under rocks,
Repelling shelter,
Favouring freedom.

The Modern Woman.

Glitter, radiance,
Superficial get-ups
A trend of the
Stiletto times.

Click, clack
Goes the heel,
Clopping along on
Platinum floors.

Out with the cash,
In with the AMEX.
Tap, tap, tap
On electronic machines.

Luster, glamour
Arched-high brows,
Glossed lips,
The modern woman.

She an icon
Contemporary, cultivated.
Rest of us Icarus
Flanking the Sun.

Secretly we wish,
She were falling.
Unzipping haphazardly
At her sown seams.

Her slim suit
Hiding her uglies.
We wish her
Our misfortunes.

Make her seem
More real, more tenable
On paper.
A blotched inky line, perhaps.

Be a wine stain
Lacking graciousness.
Instead beauty
Captivates us all.

She floats
A cloud of her own.
The author of her life
Unfair to us.

Eat less.

Exquisite and enough
The taste of
The simplest smallest
Frugal foods.

The digestive tract
Sending sultry thanks
For the consumption of
Raw and paleo.

The modern world
Eating and eating
Gusto, gluttony
Too much processed.

A certain discipline
To harken towards
Minimalism, satisfaction
With less.

Reject the pull of hormones,
Object emotions that propel to eat.
Let mind conquer body,
Do not submit to dopamine defeat.

Away from sucrose,
Fructose, starch
Lest our building blocks
Shake on sweets.

Clogging arteries
Sucking life from
Heart and Teeth, these
Deep-fried delights.

Stomach fat, arm fat
Slapped straight from
Hamburgers and cokes.
Temporary joy.

A warped slow brain
Outcome of junk.
A lackadaisical mood,
Inflated prune.

Eat greens, instead be
Spinach our salvation.
The obesity epidemic --
Shameful, wasteful.

Look to the East,
Less is more.
Simple foods anew,
A promising zeal.

Ode to Work.

My work affords me purpose.
It gives routine to my day.
It wakes me from mindless stupor,
Guilty as charged, may I say.

Perfunctory some may argue,
My movements robot-like, mundane.
Yet work saves me from nihilism,
That path too dangerous, too arcane.

Am I superficial to say I work for money,
For it equates to joy that may be bought.
My income, my greatest asset.
Without it, I am nought.

Money must work for me.
To gain it, I must not fear loss.
That is the greatest challenge,
In a world where mistakes cost.

Wealth and capital matters to others
And by extension, supposedly to me.
I am omnipresent with this awareness.
As disastrous as that may be.

This modern century gives money value,
A social currency unmatched.
A parochial egotistical pursuit,
Denial of which is dispatched.

Away with the old idealism,
That permeated my youthful days.
Incessant was I in my assertion,
That money did not me sway.

The reality is that sordid comforts,
Are afforded by the bread I make.
Without it I sleep on streets,
My power dwindling, unlike a Rake.

So like a caveman bracing for hunt,
I sharpen my tools for the next day.
Like the collective unquestioning individual,
I work silently, without a say.

Victim to Desire.

Desire is my greatest fault,
For that I am to blame.
I crave for things I cannot have,
Then I regret, full of shame.

I am impulsive in nature,
I act without a thought.
In my head the measurements fit,
But in life, I am caught.

I am restrained by my limits,
They grapple and tease me everyday.
A shove on the shoulder, a reminder
That destiny, fate is at play.

May I come to my senses,
May responsibility drag me back.
To the deep waters I once escaped,
How strange, that I want that.

The pull of oblivion,
Now less strong than before.
Desire once quaked my Earth,
Now I disregard it, por favor.

Acceptance is Key.

No stranger am I to failure,
An expert in setback.
Disappointment has plagued me,
I hope God can change that.

I study the lives of those successful,
I read and I read.
Crafting my mind's recesses,
With thoughts I hope to breed.

Like a tree with deep strong roots,
Let them take hold in my brain.
Make me an upstanding person,
With glory to my name.

Like other Type-A persons,
I compare myself with the rest.
Realise I am small in comparison,
Then close my petals, I failed the test.

In the end, I am diminutive,
In this world of legacies,
There is always a better person,
Far newer and shinier than me.

Competition then loses its meaning,
With the realisation I'll always fail.
My perspective, it needs changing.
My demons, they must bail.

To live in tranquility,
I must be at peace with the present.
Not living in a utopian future,
Nor seeking a better investment.

What is Love.

What is love, you may ask.
Is it a desire to be held.
Or perhaps it's external validation
From a source that's not yourself.

Intimacy in its many forms
It's only natural, we as humans crave.
We are, after all, intellectuals
Whose needs surpass the primitive gaze.

Physical, emotional,
Whatever the love language be
We harmonise with one another
Growing stronger as a unit, a team.

When I look inward
Deep within myself,
I see a little girl,
Wanting to be held.

I hope that for the right person,
One day I may be enough.
My broken flawed package
Wrapped in a glorified bunch.

The Distinction of Humankind.

The divine Animal Kingdom,
Predator and Prey.
They fight for survival
Whilst us humans complain.

The macaques ride on deer,
The lions bask on planes,
The penguins swim from sea lions,
Scampering mongrels happy with grains.

But the nature of human cut-throat
Gives pen more credence than sword.
We clamour to escalate ladders
We ourselves have sought.

When the Earth came into existence
It did not to us say,
That we must engineer buildings
Or craft things from clay.

Our existence is our making,
We voluntarily see to it.
So it is then by extension
Our conflict may be a gift.

Defending Daydreams.

Is it not strange how we know
In the depths of our heart
When things won't go our own way.
Yet we spite disappointment
Due to our expectations
That sky-rocket day by day.
We submerge our intuition
And ultimately think less
For thinking makes us weep.
Instead the happiness and exhilaration
That comes from living our dreams
Keeps us going despite what may.
As the notables do
We hope, imagine, create
It pushes us to move.
Without it we'd remain
In our dark dinghy taverns
Isolated, listless, not gay.
So excuse me for ignoring
The wisened old man
Who tells me to acquiesce to reality.
If I listened to him
I'd be six foot deep
Under the shrubs of my own tyranny.

Excuse the Private Person.

I ask myself time and again
Why other people seem so happy.
They broadcast their business
Without a moment's hesitation
With regards to judgment or vanity.
I, myself, am shy to share
My comings and goings with others,
In fear that when the small talk is over
My deepest truths will be a bother.
That is when the fragile shell
That is my person will come undone.
Like a crab without its outer case,
I'd become the hunted one.
So I share less, keep to myself
In hopes that I am protected.
I don't have the confidence
As my friends do,
To become a victim or a target.
Call me a coward,
The wise'd say I'm prudent,
Since the masks we wear are fake.
So what others show me,
May not actually be,
Thus my reticence is not in vain.

To be Truly Pure is a Blessing.

Why is it that when I have
What I finally wanted
That it seems too much for me,
And yet still not enough.
No matter how perfect the vessel appears,
On day two it loses its appeal.
In our minds there is always better,
A better perspective, colour, feel.
So in the end we are never happy,
We disillusion ourselves with something better.
Every moment, every hour, our thoughts change,
Perceptions influenced by our environment.
We are innately malleable,
A detriment perhaps.
We attach our being to external temporal
pleasures,
Flimsy in the wind, bending to desire.
Loss of true peace, flailing happiness.
Appreciate fine indulgences,
But practice detachment.
Dynamic push and pull,
Become the neutral omniscient observers.
Passive onlookers to the waves of the tide
Guided by the moon's forces, guided by destiny,
Looking to the stars for solace and guidance.

The Boredom of Daily Life.

Monotonous like a robot
Surging on day after day
Tired, intrepid, looking inward
Hoping for change, progression.
Heavy eyes, brewing ache behind temples
Putting myself through the motions
Pick up the drill, talk, drill, wait
Go home, sleep, repeat.
Where is the joy in life I ask,
Isolated, alone, away from everyone.
Trying to seize the moment,
Grip the present,
Be happy with the now.
So difficult, yearning for positivity.
Looking to spirituality,
Long walks outside,
Peppy music, spontaneous conversation.
Trying to find excitement in the little things.
A task I have set myself.

Does God exist.

To believe and pray to God
Is to give oneself to destiny.
Abandon with one's fears,
Abandon with one's mutiny.

Inner peace is cultivated
With spiritual endeavour.
Enemies on the battlefield,
They are made to surrender.

The going-ons come to quash,
The world halts to mute standstill.
Believe in the omniscient observer,
Become one with supposed guilt.

Close eyes, see darkness,
Rest and breathe tranquility.
Hmm and hah to a higher power,
Without him there is uncertainty.

Amor fati, Nietzsche would say
To those seeking wisdom.
Divorce oneself from thy soul
To divert oneself from ruinism.

As the Weather warms.

The sun sets in Spring
Warm, windy weather.
The glitter of stars
Emerging like balls of blowing gas.
Painting a silhouette against
The canvas of the blue sky.
A wide open expanse
Infinity, and beyond.
Shadows bouncing off luminescent tree-tops
Window panes flecked with dust.
Swirling lazy winds carrying flies,
Out come the lizards, seeking shade.
The occasional pelt of rain,
Descending on balmy roads.
Moistness, humid, sudden burst of cool.
Neither here nor there,
The mirage of Spring.

Who am I, really?

The creative element that has been my person
Has been dormant for days.
All of a sudden my imagination woken
Like a drought broken with rain.

Torrent, turbulence as this new self emerges,
Unstoppable gusto and ado.
Like bursts of bright colours splashed on white
canvas,
The previous self who withdrew.

It's almost like over the years I have sought
To squash this bug that is myself.
Why, I beg to ask
In favour of what else.

Perhaps I lacked the time,
I had to guide my thoughts to a singular focus.
I rejected what wasn't relevant
To my study, to my career, to my locus.

Like a moth to a flame, like an ant to a hill,
Drawn am I to creative thought.
In it I now covet shelter, refuge
Things that were hard-wrought.

Survival of the Fittest.

What is the key to stillness,
Wherefrom doth satisfaction ensue.
In this Western modern civilization,
I have not a single clue.

We read, we speak, we share, we reconcile.
Hoping to glean awareness and aim.
Ambition is the springboard from which we
bounce,
A novel we write, without a name.

But alas! When the light dims,
When we are left alone to our thoughts,
Squalid bitterness in the mind takes hold,
We gravitate to the Old without a cause.

And so our demons take hold,
They never let us rest.
We are caught in a poisonous cyclical pattern,
Life puts us to the test.

We must then do what we don't want,
We must conduct against our morals.
Only the fittest may survive,
Darwin's theory indeed more than wit.

So let us put up our feet then,
Devoid, nil of expectations.
There is no point in folly existence,
Neither in lame altercations.

Luxury Car.

Beamer car sitting in the garage,
Washed, shiny, new.
Waxed with the finest paint.
Not a single missing screw.

It cruises, glides along the road,
A quiet purr to its name.
When the accelerator is pressed,
It punches me back, a burning flame.

The hood hides a tasteful engine,
A sequence of intricate wires and pipes.
It spans across the front window,
Like the Sahara desert, stretching wide.

As it sits, alone, in the concrete carpark,
It draws a stare, maybe two.
Bystanders look in longing,
The car, oh so materialistic, but so blue.

Sure, it gets from A to B.
But indeed, it does more than that.
It rolls along in comfort, in style,
Sleek satisfaction, perfect, phat.

www.ingramcontent.com/pod-product-compliance
Lightning Source LLC
LaVergne TN
LVHW021352200726
843509LV00014B/2805